Affiliate Marketing Expert

Affiliate Marketing Expert

ALSO BY SPENCER COFFMAN

A Guide To Deception
Relax And Unwind
Work Less Live More
A Healthier You!

Affiliate Marketing Expert

Affiliate Marketing Expert

BY
SPENCER COFFMAN

AFFILIATE MARKETING EXPERT

First edition. June 2016.

ISBN: 978-15471945-7-5 (Paperback)
ISBN: 978-1-3704921-9-0 (Digital)
ISBN: 978-1-0942981-0-8 (Audio)

Written by Spencer Coffman.
SpencerCoffman.com

Tired Of Struggling To Make Money Online?

Discover The Simple, Step-By-Step Method To Make Thousands Of Dollars Per Month, Or More, With Affiliate Marketing!

From: Spencer Coffman

Dear Friend,

Are you looking for a proven roadmap to make a lot of money online?

Although there are all sorts of methods that you can use to make money online, many are difficult, require a lot of time and effort, or even require a substantial monetary investment.

The big reason many people fail online is because they don't make money fast enough so they give up.

To build a REAL, online business, you need to get some BIG wins very quickly.

The best way to do that is with affiliate marketing!

Affiliate Marketing Expert

- You can get started with affiliate marketing as soon as today.
- You don't have to do a bunch of market research or even create your own product or service... you get paid for promoting someone else's product.
- Getting started is as easy as choosing a market and promoting it.
- Many affiliate programs pay commissions as high as 75% That means, you're often getting paid more than the product owner.
- It's easy to quickly scale up your income to $10,000 per month or beyond!

So, if affiliate marketing is so easy, why isn't everyone making 5 or 6 figures per month or beyond?

To Succeed With Affiliate Marketing, You MUST Consider...

- Finding the right affiliate products to promote.
- How to get approved for the affiliate offers that you want to promote.
- Getting everything setup the right way without wasting time and spinning your wheels.
- How to get online traffic easily and start promoting your first affiliate product while making a profit.
- Tracking everything so you know when to scale a campaign up and take it to the next level.

Most People That Try
Affiliate Marketing... Fail.

Why?

Not because it's hard, but because they try to "wing it" and just figure it all out.

In many cases, they look at free resources that may be outdated or simply don't work.

Many people that try to figure things out on their own with affiliate marketing end up losing money...

Although it's hard to put a price on **NOT** losing money and **NOT** wasting time, that's exactly what you're getting when you make the wise decision to take action today!

The Key To Success With
Affiliate Marketing Is In The Details...

To see success with affiliate marketing and make the kind of money that you want to make, you need to follow a proven roadmap to online success.

You need to "plug-in" to a tried and tested method that has been used before!

Not someone that was seeing results last year or the

year before...
Someone that knows what's working TODAY!

Introducing:
Affiliate Marketing Expert

Inside This Step-By-Step Guide To Making Money With Affiliate Marketing, You'll Discover...

- How to get started even if you've never made a penny online.
- The fastest way to begin earning up to $10k per year with affiliate marketing and how to scale that up to $100k per year or more!
- The best products to promote as an affiliate and how to find them.
- The two options you have when it comes to generating traffic to your offers and how to get started.
- How to build an audience that will buy the offers you put in front of them and make you the most money possible.
- The BEST platforms for finding products that pay high commissions.
- Why focusing on a big niche might not always be the best way.
- The ultimate beginner's strategy to get started and make a profit.
- What you need to do to boost sales quickly.
- Two simple online methods for quickly making sales.

- How to leverage your existing network to quickly take your affiliate marketing business to six figures and beyond!
- A simple strategy for making commissions in everyday life…
- How to use content marketing online to build a massive following.
- Why paid marketing can often be one of the fastest ways to profit.
- The secrets that ALL successful affiliate marketers must follow.
- Plus, a whole lot more!

At this point, it's obvious that affiliate marketing is one of the fastest ways to start making money online.

Yes! I really want to learn how I can start making huge affiliate commissions online starting as soon as today!

So please send me my copy of "Affiliate Marketing Expert" so I can build my online business to start making money right away!

Claim Your Copy Today!

Affiliate Marketing Expert

Affiliate Marketing Expert

Affiliate Marketing Expert

Table of Contents

Chapter 1:

The Life of an Affiliate Marketer: What to Expect

If you're looking to make a ton of money online, then the best option for the widest selection of people is undoubtedly affiliate marketing. This is the online business model with the fewest barriers to entry that anyone can learn and anyone can master. At the same time, it is potentially one of the most profitable business models you can use online and is certainly much more profitable than blogging for AdSense revenue, or some other similar market.

Affiliate Marketing Expert

The fact that it is much more profitable than blogging is a point that advertisers on Facebook love to present. Chances are that you have already seen millions of advertisements for online money making schemes and 'programs'. You may not have recognized them as such, but nevertheless, they were there all along. The crazy fact is, that nine out of ten times, those ads are solely based around affiliate marketing.

You'll know these ads when you see them. It is the type of advertisement where people talk to you from their private yacht and tell you how they make a 6-figure salary in only a few hours of work each week. It is the type of ad that sounds too good to be true. Often times, they are written off as a pyramid scheme or some form of multi-level marketing.

In addition, you have probably have seen the videos of online 'billionaires' talking about their money-making systems while wearing smart suits in very pimped-out offices. They've created a 'digital empire' all on their own using affiliate marketing techniques, and now they're rich and powerful and you probably want to be them…

But is this all true? Can you really accomplish all that through affiliate marketing? Is it really that easy? Or is there more to it than that?

Well, I'll tell you right now, so that you don't read the whole book waiting for the answer. Unfortunately, the answer is not a simple yes or no. It is both. First off, most of the billionaires out there with their private yachts claiming that they make tons of money from working only a few hours a week are probably telling the truth. The part they leave out is how many hours they had to work before they were able to only work a few hours a week. Yes, you can make tons of money with affiliate marketing. It is a very safe and reliable business to get into. You don't have to worry about it being a pyramid scheme or some form of multi-level marketing. It is much more than that.

Affiliate marketing is your own personal business where you earn as much, or as little, as you want. It is pretty much a commission-based job. You promote someone's product and they pay you. The more you promote, the more you make. It is that easy. So when you see all of those ads telling you that you can become rich. Remember, that you can become rich. But you won't "get rich quick". It will take a detailed plan, some time, and an investment. You need to be committed to success, and willing to see the big picture. Luckily, you have found this book. That means you are already dedicated and willing to put in some time and effort into building your business.

You have made a wise choice because, in this book, you are going to learn lots of valuable information that took years of time and experience. You are going to have a leg up on millions of people who are also trying out affiliate marketing. The information in this book is written based on years of trial and error in affiliate marketing. Fortunately, I have the kinks worked out, and know what works and what doesn't work, and I'm willing to share that information with you. Therefore, get ready, grab your notepad, and read on. This book is going to be your number one guide to making your affiliate marketing business a success. So read on, and good luck!

How Much Does an Affiliate Marketer Make?

First of all, let's assess the claims about earnings. We don't have to guess at this because there are real-life conventions for affiliate marketers that collect and report data. During the 2014 Affiliate Summit, over 1,800 affiliate marketers answered a survey describing everything from their methods to their earnings.

How much were they bringing in?

Well, only 46% earned less than $20K while 8% earned $50K-$100K and 12% earned $100K+. At the very least, this shows it's certainly very possible to earn big money. (The rest were around the middle, but note that 19% elected not to answer at all.) Therefore, it is clear that you can make some money and the idea of having your own yacht is very achievable.

What's also interesting here, though, is the sheer spread of earnings. Affiliate marketing is bringing in from $20K to $100K and beyond, which is something that you don't find in traditional careers. The reason for this spread is because some people work harder on their affiliate marketing business than other people. It is like anything, the more practice and effort you put into it, the more you will get out of it.

However, it is a lot more than simply effort. There are many large factors that go into the reasons behind this data. So what's the big difference?

It's the skill of the individual.

As an affiliate marketer, you're self-employed and working alone. There's no need to 'climb the corporate ladder' or to compete for promotions. You can get to the top overnight if you have the right skills because it's all on you. In addition, you have to have the self-determination and the self-discipline to make it work. You need to be motivated to work hard and spend those long hours building your business. No one else is going to do it for you. This book will help you get started, and other online resources can help you get ideas. However, the implementation is all on you. You need to put the time into it because you will reap what you sow. This book is your owner's manual and guide. It isn't going to make you rich. You are going to make you rich by applying what you will learn in this book.

The Affiliate Marketing Lifestyle: What Does Affiliate Marketing Involve?

Perhaps the biggest draw of affiliate marketing though is not the money. Instead, for many people, the appeal lies in the fact that this is a completely 'passive' business model. Once you've set everything up, such as your sales funnel, your affiliate network account, and your blog/sales page, then you can literally earn money while you're sleeping, or while you're on vacation.

Another draw to the affiliate marketing business is that you are entirely your own boss. People in today's world are tired of working for the man. They want to be free. People today are hungry for a lifestyle where they answer to no one but themselves. They want to break out of the everyday mundane life of working all day long for nothing. People want to make money and be their own boss so that they can be free to do what they want when they want. Therefore, affiliate marketing is very appealing to a lot of people. However, it isn't as easy as people think it is, or make it out to be.

But again, this can get twisted. The freedom that people seek when they get into affiliate marketing doesn't come overnight. It comes after a lot of hard work and determination. But it will pay off! You've seen the statistics. The money is there, it is simply a question of whether or not you are going to earn your share. Because the truth of the matter is that affiliate marketing is likely to initially involve a lot of work. The idea here is that you put in the work up front so that you can sow the seeds of your labor further down the line. To begin with, you need to be willing to put in a lot of hours for very little reward. The dominoes must be set up before you can achieve the enjoyment of watching them fulfill their purpose.

Specifically then, what does affiliate marketing involve?

If you're reading this book, then there's a good chance

you have a general idea, but we'll recap in a little more detail for those who do not.

Essentially, as an affiliate marketer, you sell products for a commission. This means you'll be finding products online and promoting them using your own affiliate link. If someone clicks on your link and then buys the product, or, in some cases, any product on that website, you'll get a cut of the profit. Often times, you can expect your cut to be as much as 50% all the way up to 75% of the retail price.

One huge advantage of affiliate marketing is that there's no risk involved for you. This goes for more than one aspect. First, is because you're not creating the product. You don't have anything investing in creation, promotion, marketing, et cetera. In addition, there's nothing for you to ship, or for you to store. You don't need to spend time housing inventory or packaging items. All you have to do is sell and you earn more than the creator! How about that for a deal!!! Sounds too good to be true, but it isn't. Believe me, there are reasons.

The hard part lies within doing the selling. This is where the 'marketing' part comes in. Your job from here is to find yourself a large audience through a blog, through an e-mail campaign, through advertising, through social media, or whichever tool you find the most effective. The point is, you need to find yourself a very large audience that will follow you, and click on the links you promote. That way you can earn an affiliate commission.

This is why there's no steep learning curve or a barrier to entry for beginners. It is something that you can simply set up and it will begin working for you. All you're literally doing is making sure people see your affiliate link. There's no product creation and no investment. You can get started tomorrow, in minutes, and it won't cost you a penny. All you need is a plan.

If you're a big blogger, and you already have an audience of 10,000 readers a day then you're going to find this very easy. All you need to do is put some very persuasive text on your website along with the link and you'll start driving traffic instantly. Which means you'll start earning huge affiliate commissions in only a few days. On the other hand, if you don't have a large following, and you're new at affiliate marketing, then you may find this process a little more complex and little more daunting.

You now have two options:

Build your own audience – OR – Advertise

(Actually, there are other methods and growth hacks you can use which we'll come to later, but for now, this will suffice.)

Advertising

If you're going to use the route of paid marketing, then that means you're going likely going to be using PPC. This is 'Pay Per Click' and it basically means that you pay for every person who clicks on your ad and thus gets sent to your site. The more you pay, the more visitors you get. Google AdWords is probably the most popular Pay Per Click service. It is an effective form of marketing that winds up driving a lot of traffic. The trouble is, that not all clicks result in a sale. The goal is to not only get enough affiliate sales to cover the cost of your PPC campaigns but also to receive additional sales that you wouldn't otherwise receive.

If you design your site well, and you can really convince people to buy your products, then you should be able to convert a predictable amount of visitors into buyers. This, in turn, means you can work out the exact return on your investment. Find out what you're spending on your Pay Per Click campaign and divide that number by your total visitors driven as a result of that campaign. That will tell you exactly how much you are paying for each visitor. Therefore, if you pay a certain amount per visitor, and a certain amount of those visitors earn you a certain amount of money, then you can tell whether or not your strategy is profitable.

The amount you pay per click will depend on the amount of competition available for your ad. Pay Per Click ads work on a 'bidding' system, whereby the advertiser offering the most per click is the advertiser whose ads are most likely to show up in the search results.

Meanwhile, even if your website is very effective at convincing people to buy, you'll still only get about 1%-10% of visitors converting (and more often, you'll be at the bottom end of that spectrum). So you'll need your ad to be seen by about 1,000-2,000 people in order for you to get a single sale, which means you'll be paying a relatively high amount for your ad to be seen by 10,000 to 20,000 times for about 100 sales. If your average affiliate sale is $20 then that means you will earn about $1,000 for every 10,000 to 20,000 times your ad is seen.

This is a formula that takes a lot of adjusting and you can expect to lose a certain amount of money before you get it right. However, once you have it down to a science, you can expect to be making some pretty good money through your Pay Per Click service. The trouble is, that the return on your investment is relatively low.

With a good set-up, you can expect to spend $600 a day on a Pay Per Click service to make about $200 profit. That's a pretty big risk, especially when you're first starting out. Add that to the fact that for the first few months you probably will be operating at a loss (until you learn the right keywords to target, the right products to sell, the right sales pitch et cetera), and the reward for your risk doesn't really seem worth it.

Pay Per Click has a lot of potential to work out. However, it will work a lot better if you already have a huge audience that is dedicated to following you. If they like your content then they will be more apt to click on your links and will, therefore, be more likely to purchase the products you promote. That means that you will make more money on your investment. Therefore, unless you have tons of religious followers, Pay Per Click might not be for you. Which means that you have another option. Essentially, it is the first step. You should do this before you embark on a Pay Per Click campaign. That step is explained next.

Building an Audience

If you don't have that kind of money to play around with, then your only other option is to build your audience naturally over time. In case you didn't get that last part here it is again. Over Time. You need to build your audience over time, and then use that audience to receive affiliate sales.

That means creating a blog and then using it to promote yourself through social media and build up a mailing list full of subscribers. Again, you can't expect your initial conversion rate to be all that high. In addition, you're going to need about 10,000 views daily to make even close to a full-time living.

Getting to this point is slow going. You can expect it to take at least a year before receiving 600 visitors a day and while you'll accumulate exponential growth at this point, it will still likely be a few years before you're at 10,000 visitors a day.

Oh, and at this point, affiliate marketing is anything but passive. At this stage in the game, you'll be investing huge amounts of time into writing a compelling blog that people will want to follow. You'll also be constantly emailing your subscribers and managing your advertising campaigns. This is the middle road of your path to becoming rich.

It won't be long until you can set up your blog to automatically retrieve content so that you won't need to be spending time writing anymore. You'll also have all of your emails set up to automatically be sent out with each new post. That is your goal, completely automated affiliate marketing. You simply work a few hours a week performing maintenance and let the followers and clicks roll in. It is very possible to be highly successful at affiliate marketing. You definitely can earn hundreds of thousands of dollars from it, and once you're all set up, the money will come in while you sleep.

However, it also requires a big upfront investment of time and/or money, depending on which of the two methods you go with. In addition, you also need the right know-how and strategy. If it didn't take time, then everyone would be rich, no one would work for an employer, and the economy would collapse. However, for those who are dedicated, affiliate marketing can be an extremely profitable line of work.

So it's a good thing really...

Those who want it can achieve it. Those who think they want it, will try it and then give up. Which person are you?

How to Approach Affiliate Marketing

The last section wasn't intended to depress you and hopefully, you haven't put the book/tablet down and abandoned all hope at this point. It was simply a reality check. The last section was because I want to make sure that you fully understand what it is going to take for you to be successful in the affiliate marketing business. There is no fluff no muff, only the honest truth.

All it means is that you need to set out with not only the right approach but also the right expectations. Don't go into affiliate marketing thinking you'll be a millionaire overnight because you'll only be sorely disappointed and this will lead to your giving up. Instead, understand that this is a slow process and that, to begin with, it's not going to be your sole income.

The way you can get around this is to make affiliate marketing into somewhat of a hobby on top of your regular job. Or you can set up some different business model in order to earn the money you need to invest into affiliate marketing.

This might seem like a lot of work, but if you can find the time outside of your regular job to upload three articles per week and do a little bit of marketing, you should be able to make some steady progress. Three hours a week will most likely be enough to get started. While you won't be rich, the rewards for this will still be impressive.

Let's say you start making one sale a week at $40 profit. You're not paying for advertising, but rather building your blog organically. This now means you're making an additional $160 a month. That, in turn, is an impressive $1,920 a year on top of your regular salary.

Affiliate Marketing Expert

This is enough to purchase a nice computer, to invest in some helpful software, some website investments, Pay Per Click, or even a little vacation.

If you faithfully upload your three articles each week and spend the time placing effective affiliate links then this will accelerate pretty fast. It won't be long until you start earning $3,000 or $4,000 over the year. Even if you never progress beyond that point, you've now increased your annual salary and you can now live a different lifestyle. Keep at it with dedication and perseverance and you will be well on your way to earning an extra $10,000 or more every year.

You'll have financial security in case you ever find yourself unemployed. What's more, if you've chosen to sell products in a niche that you're interested in, then you'll be able to enjoy yourself while doing all this. Not only will you be building a large audience, but you will also enjoy becoming an authority figure in an area that you love. Keep it up and eventually, you can start earning millions while you sleep.

However, make sure that this isn't your initial goal. As you begin, your goal should be to earn some nice supplementary income. Then, eventually, earn enough to replace your regular income. This might sound trivial, but it really isn't. Starting out with the right expectations and intentions will be the difference between giving up and enjoying a great career that will eventually set you free.

That is the first, and most important, 'secret' to affiliate marketing. But the rest are going to help you accelerate your progress with growth hacks and other techniques. This way, you won't have to wait all that long until you start making the progress that likely attracted you to affiliate marketing in the first place. Instead of taking ten years to start making an excellent income. You will hopefully be able to do it in three to five.

Affiliate Marketing Expert

Chapter 2:

The Mechanics of Affiliate Marketing: How it All Works

At this point, you should understand how affiliate marketing works and what it is going to take for you to be successful. Now you are ready to learn about the precise mechanics involved in affiliate marketing and how understanding this can help you to be more effective at your job.

What happens, for example, when someone clicks on one of your affiliate links?

Affiliate Marketing Expert

The answer is 'cookies'. If you browse the Internet at all, you probably know what cookies are. However, in case you don't fully understand what they do, here is a description. Cookies are small files that get saved on your computer and are handled by your browser. Websites can store cookies and then look for them on your computer when you access the site at a later time. Cookies help the site load faster, keep you logged into Facebook, or show you relevant advertisements based on your browsing history.

When a buyer clicks on your link, they get sent to the checkout page for a specific product. At the same time though, a cookie will be stored on their computer, which will identify them as having been referred by you. This means that when they make a purchase, the profits can be allocated to you. In some cases, cookies can be saved on a computer for 30, 60, or even 90 days. That is if the computer owner doesn't clear them, of course. That means that if you have a certain type of software, app, or plugin on your affiliate site, then you can set your cookies to be stored on someone's computer for days. That way, anytime they revisit that site, even if they don't click on your link, you will still get credit for the sale. Pretty cool huh?

It is very important for you to grasp the concept of cookies and fully understand it. A large portion of buyers may know that you will be credited for referring them and they may avoid clicking on your link. In addition, they may not want cookies stored on their computer. Therefore, they may see your ads and then simply go to their favorite shopping site and find the product on their own. This is called 'link bypassing' and it's worth your while to prevent this using link cloaking.

Link cloaking is a very powerful tool that will allow you to post your affiliate links on all kinds of social media sites without the site recognizing that it is an affiliate link. This is very valuable because most social media sites prohibit posting affiliate links. Another great advantage of link cloaking is that it will considerably shorten your URL. Many affiliate links can be several hundred characters, especially eBay and Amazon links. Therefore, if you cloak them, you can have normal links that are easy for people to read and remember. In some cases, you can even choose your own custom link.

There are several different ways that you can cloak links, all of which involve the use of a service. Some of these services provide cloaking free of charge, and others make you pay for it. Beware of the services that provide free cloaking. In some cases, they may be converting your affiliate link to their own so that they get credit for the sale instead of you. A couple of the more popular link cloaking services are TinyURL and Bit.ly. Hootsuite also offers link cloaking and Amazon offers a shortened URL. Of these four, Amazon will definitely not steal your affiliate link. TinyURL and Bit. ly should be safe. Hootsuite may or may not convert your link depending on the type of account you have.

The best way to avoid any question of whether or not you are being credited with your affiliate link is to code your own links. Unfortunately, this is not an option for most people because they don't know code. Fortunately, here is a sample code that you can use to cloak your link.

```
<meta http-quiv="refresh" content="0; url=http://www.example.com/affiliatelink">
```

However, this can become very complicated and time-consuming. In addition, it may not always work out for you. Therefore, I have found that the absolute best way to cloak your links is to use a plugin called PrettyLink. It is a simple WordPress plugin that you can install on your website or blog. You are then able to paste in any affiliate link you want and choose your own custom URL for that link. For example, if you have a link for an iPhone you can set your affiliate URL to be "yoursite.com/iphone".

This is a huge advantage because not only will it drive traffic and recognition to your domain name, but any social media site will accept your post. It will also let your readers know exactly what they are going to see when they click the link. Another great advantage of this plugin is that you can put your links directly in YouTube videos as long as you associate your website with your channel. PrettyLink basically creates a link that people will see as belonging to your website. Then, instead of a page on your website loading, readers will be redirected to your affiliate site. In case you haven't noticed, I highly recommend using PrettyLink.

There is both a free, Lite, version and a paid, Pro, version, both of which are excellent. Of course, if you are really serious about affiliate marketing I highly recommend the paid version because it has so many more options. In addition, at the writing of this book, it is only a one-time purchase of either $47 for the Blogger Edition or $97 for the Developer Edition and you will have lifetime access. I recommend the Developer Edition because you can use it on an unlimited number of websites. This is crucial because even though you may only have one website or blog now, you will most likely have more in the future. Why buy the Blogger Edition and then a year from now you want to upgrade. Perhaps by then, they are charging a monthly fee. Now you have no choice but to pay it or find something else. Keep it simple, and eliminate the future hassle. $97 isn't that much for a plugin that actually works like it is supposed to work.

Hopefully, you noticed that I spent more time discussing PrettyLink than any other link cloaking service. That is your first tip. You have now learned something in ten minutes that took me almost a year to figure out. Therefore, if, throughout this book, you notice that I spend a lot of time on one particular product it means that that product works and you need to get it if you want to make your affiliate marketing life easier. Therefore, buy PrettyLink because it works and because you need it. Not because I told you to do so.

Another thing to keep in mind regarding cookies is that you need to do a little research into the affiliate scheme that you're going to be working with. That's because the creator of a cookie is the one who sets the lifespan, not you. As mentioned earlier, a cookie can last a few minutes, or it can last until the user actively chooses to delete their cookies from their computer. You want to have a cookie last as long as possible because the longer a cookie is on someone's computer, the better chance you have of making an affiliate sale.

Of course, it's much better for you to have an affiliate scheme with cookies that don't expire at all. Amazon has a 'session limited' cookie scheme for instance that only lasts 24 hours. That's actually pretty good in this case though, considering that people already know about Amazon and you can make money from other things people buy from the site that day. However, some Amazon store builders have cookies that last for 90 days. That means that whatever someone purchases on Amazon within that 90 day period is all attributed to you.

The only thing that you have to worry about with your cookies is whether or not a subsequent affiliate can 'override' your cookie. This becomes relevant if someone should click your affiliate link, not make a purchase, then click someone else's affiliate link and buy. Who gets the money? This depends on whether the affiliate honors the first click or last click. If you are a 'lifetime referrer' then you will always be given credit for the referral regardless of what else happens subsequently.

However, when you are first starting out, if someone clicks on another link after clicking on your link then you are out of luck. Generally, it is best not to lose your head over this because it is pretty much out of your control. All you need to worry about is cloaking your links and trying to find a link with the longest lasting cookies possible. In reality, the most important thing is the link. Cookies are less important. You want to have a link so that people can click on it. Worry about the cookies later.

Types of Affiliate Programs and Choosing the Best Product

With those technical details out the way, it's time to start choosing affiliate products and schemes. The first step here is deciding which type of affiliate scheme you want to join. There are three basic types of affiliate schemes that you can join. All of them are online, and they all involve driving sales to a particular item. The question is whether you want to sell a digital product, a physical product, or a service?

Digital products are exactly that. They are things that are online and are intangible goods. Digital products can include but are not limited to, music, movies, eBooks, plugins, apps, software, et cetera. Physical products are tangible goods. They are products that must be physically shipped out to the buyer. Physical product affiliate sales involve companies like Amazon, eBay, Overstock, Wal-Mart, et cetera. Services are a little trickier. Of course, there are many sites that perform services that you can promote. The most common one is probably Fiverr. Basically, someone needs something done; this something usually involves some form of computer work, like coding, file conversion, editing, et cetera. You promote their service and they pay you.

Affiliate Marketing Expert

This is probably the most difficult form of affiliate marketing because there is a select audience. The only sales here are sales from people who seek out the service. There are no impulse buys, like with digital and physical products. Therefore, it would be better for you to avoid this area, unless you have a service oriented blog or website.

The best area to get into, for most beginners, is digital product affiliate marketing. There's no cost associated with production, storage, or delivery and because of this, the product creator gets a much bigger slice of the profit. That means that they have more profit to share with you. This, in turn, means that you can earn even more from each affiliate sale. I recommend starting out promoting digital products and then adding physical products so that your site is evenly balanced. Physical products are easy to find. Simply go to Amazon, eBay, or any other online retailer and sign up for the affiliate program. Digital products can be a little more involved but remember they produce a higher profit margin.

To find digital products, you need to look at different affiliate networks such as JVZoo, ClickBank, Commission Junction, Trade Bit, or Warrior Forum Special Offers.

To use one of these sites, all you need to do is sign up, browse through the available products, and then apply to work as an affiliate for a few of them. You can see data and information about each one, such as the number of sales, the cost, affiliate commission, refund rate, conversion rate, et cetera.

From there, you want to choose a digital product that is making a lot of sales and has a pretty low refund rate. In addition, you also want one that offers you a good amount of cash per sale. Try to find an affiliate that will pay you 60% or greater. Many affiliates will even pay you 80%! Think about how you're going to market each of those products, and what 'angle' you'll go with to make it desirable for your audience.

Trying out the product is a very good idea, as is finding one that offers free marketing materials that the product creator designed. Some will come with free landing pages, blog posts, email autoresponder sequences, and more that you can utilize. If a product doesn't come with free bonuses, it can be a good idea to add your own. Simply find some worthwhile PDF documents or tutorial courses related to the product you are promoting. Then offer those free to people if they purchase the product. These free products will hopefully help entice your potential buyers into becoming real buyers. It will also help them to feel more satisfied with their purchase because they are receiving so much "free stuff" with their purchase.

Promoting digital products means you make more money per sale and it means there's less that can go wrong. It's also the preferred method by many digital marketers, which means you'll find a lot more advice and help. As mentioned before, this is a great way to start out. It is very easy to do and can be very profitable. Some good ways to begin promoting digital products are to write reviews on certain products and then add your affiliate link to the review. Post the reviews on your website, social media, YouTube, and wherever else you can. I highly recommend starting out with digital products. Then once you get signed up for the different sites, have your game plan, and have your links in place; you can move onto physical products.

However, some people feel more comfortable selling physical products because they don't really grasp the concept of digital products. That is perfectly fine. Keep in mind, that if this is you, then eventually, you need to move into digital products as well. It is very important to have your hand in both physical and digital products. Unless your website or blog is specifically orientated towards one of those particular schemes, that is. Physical products can be found by signing up with Amazon Associates, eBay Partner Network, Clickbank, Commission Junction, or any other online retailer that offers an affiliate program. People like selling physical products because they have a very wide audience, and impulse buys make up more than half of the sales. In addition, only certain types of people are interested in eBooks, software, and other digital items whereas music, movies, apps, and those types of digital items are popular for everyone.

On the other hand, we all spend money on physical items. After all, pretty much everyone is interested in cell phone accessories, clothing items, or whatever the product may be. This means you have a much larger potential audience.

Unfortunately, though, physical products also cost a lot more to produce. Not only are there more production costs, there is also shipping, packaging, labor, and all of the legal channels that they must go through before being on the market. When you sell a product through Amazon, for instance, the money is going to get split between you, the product creator, Amazon, the delivery company, and possibly even another reseller. That's a lot of division for a $10 to $20 product.

Basically, affiliates on Amazon tend to get roughly 4-8% per sale as opposed to 50-75% per sale for digital products. The products will also often be cheaper and less geared toward getting digital sales. Why would someone click your link to buy a computer when they can simply go to their local technology store? These are the considerations you'll need to take into account when you start trying to sell physical products rather than digital products.

Physical products can be tough because people can simply go to their local Wal-Mart to buy what they need, whereas digital products are only available online. Therefore, you have a much better chance of making a sale. Of course, there's nothing to stop you from selling both types of product, and it is a good idea to do so. That way you will appeal to both types of people.

Ultimately, it makes more sense to start with digital products because you can make a bigger earning from fewer sales. When you're not yet getting the sheer volume of visitors you need to make hundreds of sales, selling digital products is still the quicker route to making more money. Then, once you have the digital links set up, start adding physical product links. This will supplement your site and attract more visitors. It will also help your income if they start clicking on links and purchase items.

Finally, you can look at selling services or memberships. These will often provide you with what are known as 'lifetime commissions'. For instance, if you can get people to sign up to a gambling site, eBook club, music download, Hulu, et cetera then you might be able to earn commission from them for the lifetime of their membership. Not only will you earn an affiliate commission on their initial purchase, you will also earn a commission on their monthly membership, and, in some cases, any extra funds that they spend. Get enough of these and you can be set for life, but of course, there are unique challenges here as well.

There are far fewer of these sorts of affiliate schemes and normally the best way to find them is to visit the sites in person. That means you need to be doing a lot of research to find the most popular membership sites. Unfortunately, many membership sites, like dating sites, don't have affiliate programs. That means you must contact each site to see if you can work out some sort of deal with them. Often times they will because they want their site promoted. Offering you an affiliate commission means they don't need to spend money on an advertising campaign. If you end up successfully promoting their site then it is good for both of you. If it doesn't work out, then they aren't out anything.

One hassle with this is that you may have to sign up

for an account on each of these sites individually. That means you can end up with lots of separate accounts and, in turn, things can get a little fiddly. This is more complex, and perhaps not a great starting point for beginners. In general, I recommend avoiding this method of digital sales. If you are interested in membership affiliate marketing, then find some ClickBank links to promote. They often have memberships on there for which you can become an affiliate.

Some More Tips for Choosing Your Affiliate Product

Something else to consider when choosing an affiliate product is whether it's something you will be able to sell. Not only must it be possible to sell generally, but you also need to be able to sell it personally. That means that ideally, it should be on a topic that you find interesting and that you know how to sell. It needs to be something that you like and that you will stand behind. If you are selling a product that you love, your customers will see that passion and they, too, will become enthused about the product.

When creating a blog, or building a mailing list, you will usually need to write a lot of blog posts and send many e-mails on the topic of the product in order to build trust, provide value, and offer a reason for people to come to your website in the first place. If you aren't careful, and you choose a subject you know nothing about, you'll quickly find this tiring, boring, and you'll be more likely to quit. What's more, is that readers will be able to tell that you aren't an expert on the subject which will undermine the points you make and leave your readers less inclined to trust you. They will also notice that you aren't very enthused about the product. Believe me, they will notice. People want to read an article that fires them up. They want to be excited to buy it.

Consider Billy Mays, who sold Oxy Clean. Watch one of his commercials and you will understand exactly what type of passion and enthusiasm you need to convey when selling your product. If you can follow his example, and write your posts with his form of excitement, then you will definitely have much more success with your sales.

In addition, you need to think about the advantages that are unique to you, such as any routes to market you might have. A route to market is any direct link you have with a potential audience, such as a blog or a magazine. If you already have a blog, then, of course, you need to choose a product that your readers will find interesting. On the other hand, if you have a lot of subscribers on your YouTube channel about "XYZ", then find a product that corresponds to the content on your channel. Make a video about it and use PrettyLink to send viewers directly to the sales page.

Also think about your contacts, Facebook friends, LinkedIn connections, or any of your social media acquaintances. Do any of them have thousands of connections, write for a blog, magazine, or something else? If you don't know, then find out. Take advantage of your connection to them and spread your product.

You need to take a good look at every possible sales outlet that you can think of. In what ways are you connected with people and how can you get your product in front of them. Chances are that you are already set up with thousands of potential followers. You simply need to let them know that you are ready for them to follow you. If they already know you, then they probably will. They may not purchase from you, but if they follow you, then they help boost your numbers, which helps your credibility.

It all basically boils down to choosing a product that you already know you can sell and putting that product in front of an audience that you already have. Then use your current connections to grow your audience. Even if you don't have a direct route to market, think about what the best routes to market for each product might be, and how you could go about reaching them. Don't choose a product then think about how you'll sell it, choose the product because you know you can sell it. We'll be talking more about this later in the book.

Big Niche, Little Niche

Another consideration you will have is whether to pick a 'big niche' or a 'little niche'. A 'niche' is simply the industry in which you are selling. For example, if you're selling an eBook on getting abs, your niche, and your industry, is 'fitness'. On the other hand, if you're selling an eBook on making money online, then your niche is online business. A 'big niche' is a niche that is hot and trending. It will have tons of products, lots of interested people, and lots of other affiliate marketers. A 'little niche' is a niche that may not have as widespread of a following, may not be as well known, is more specialized, and will have fewer affiliate marketers.

Making money online is the biggest niche you'll find when it comes to digital products. In fact, WSOPro (Warrior Forum Special Offers) is entirely dedicated to digital marketing products. Right after digital marketing, are the fitness niche and the online dating niche. These are great niches to get into because they are proven niches. People are happy to spend money to make money and they'll also spend money to look and feel better or to find love. These are also subjects that appeal to everyone. So if you're looking for a product with a proven track record, it will likely be in these areas.

The advantage of getting into a big niche is that you have a very large potential audience. However, you also have a lot of competition, so you need to make sure that you have top of the line posts, marketing, and products. It also helps to have lots of credibility. In addition, these areas are highly competitive and oversaturated simply because they are so popular. If you want to reach this audience then you're going to need to spend more money on Pay Per Click advertising, as you'll be bidding against more competitors. Likewise, if you want to create a blog, you'll be competing with a much larger number of other blogs for the top spot on Google, and for readers.

The advantage of a little niche is that you have less

competition and your audience is specialized so they know that they want to buy what you have. The disadvantage is that your potential audience is much smaller than that of a big niche. However, this can be a good option for people starting out. It can help build your credibility and ranking. For example, if you create a blog on 'Super Meat Boy' then you'll be among maybe two other fan sites and you'll find that you can very quickly get seen by pretty much your entire audience. Likewise, you'll probably be able to pay to advertise on Google or Facebook for these terms without spending much money. The same goes for writing about a specific job or profession. If you're selling an eBook on 'stage lighting techniques' then you'll find it much easier to reach those professionals without spending vast amounts of money.

Another option is to choose an affiliate product that aims at a smaller cross section of a much larger niche. For example, 'fitness people over 50' is a much smaller chunk of the larger 'fitness' niche. The same goes for 'digital marketing for students'. However, another important factor to consider is who your target demographic is, and, more specifically, how much disposable income they have. In this regard, aiming at people over fifty makes more sense than aiming at students!

So, which type of niche is best to get into?

The best strategy is to start smaller and then to build your way up to reach the bigger niches. Go ahead and read that again, because, that my friends, is a valuable tip that took me years to figure out. **Start small, and**

then grow.

It is a very simple concept. After all, everything starts small and grows, humans, plants, animals, businesses, et cetera. Do you think Microsoft, Apple, or Wal-Mart started with 50 buildings and millions of dollars in products? No. They all started somewhere small and grew. That is the natural rate of progression. Therefore, if you want to have a successful affiliate marketing business, then you need to follow the natural rate of progression. Don't start big and then wonder why it isn't working. It isn't working because you are doing something that is unnatural. You are going against the grain, paddling up river, walking against the wind. Get the picture?!

When you start out as an affiliate marketer, you want to be successful. Human nature is overreaching and you will want to dive into the most popular topics you can and try to sell the hottest topics that are out there. Resist this urge, because it will cripple your business. The reason is, that you will end up losing so many followers and sales. Unless you are already a seasoned pro, your blog, posts, affiliate ads, et cetera will not look as good as the other big niche ads. Therefore, viewers will skip over your content and opt for the more appealing content. When they do this, Google will track all of the people leaving your site and your bounce rate will spike. In turn, your Google ranking will tank. That means you will be buried in the search results. Then, once you get some excellent ads, posts, et cetera. They won't be found because you have already shot yourself in the foot and buried your results.

Therefore, start with a niche that only has a few other competitors. Then, review their sites, ads, and blog posts. Make your posts better than theirs. Keyword them, fill them with exciting ads, and great content. Then, you will be the best in your niche. Google will notice that viewers are leaving other people's sites to go to your site. As a result, your ranking will spike. You will be at the top of the search results for your keywords. Then, after a few months of being at the top, gradually expand your product line. Add a new niche to your existing site. Wait a few more months. Then add another niche. Then, after about a year of being at the top of the search results in three or four different little niches, you will be ready to expand to a big niche.

Important Note: It will most likely be about eighteen months to two years before you are ready to dive into a big niche. It will take you a few months to get a game plan, a few months to get all of your content looking good, a few months to climb the search rankings, and a couple more months to start converting visitors into sales. Then you'll add new niches every few months until you are ready for a big niche. Therefore, plan for eighteen months minimum. Unless you are already a professional blog writer with thousands of followers, then start with related products.

Why do Product Creators on Digital Affiliate Networks Give Away So Much Profit?

Affiliate Marketing Expert

Something you might be asking yourself at this point is why a digital product manufacturer would be willing to give away 75% of his or her profits to anyone that makes an affiliate sale. What's in it for them? Why would they only want to keep 25% of their profit when they did all of that hard work to create a product?

To understand this, it's worth considering the power of scaling up. Scaling up is a concept of exponential growth. Basically, if you have enough people selling multiple copies of your product, then you will be making more than enough sales to still become very wealthy. Sure, the creator is only making 25% per sale, but if they have 20 affiliates selling 100 copies of their item a day, they're still going to make far more than any of those individual affiliates. More importantly, they'll be able to earn much much more than they would by selling the product on their own.

Consider the math. If I create a product with a price of $10, and you become an affiliate for me, you will make $7.50 and I'll make $2.50. Now, if you sell 100 copies a day then you'll make $750 and I'll make $250. Now, if I have 10 affiliates all selling 100 copies a day, I'm making $2500 a day and each affiliate is only making $750 a day.

The more commission the affiliates offer, the more people will come on board (versus other products) and that means they'll be able to continually scale up their profits. And anyway, they're probably still making money from their own marketing activities where they'll be making 100% per sale. The sales they get from affiliates are all on top of the earnings from their own marketing efforts.

Basically, the goal of any creator is to get their product out there. If they are a good, worthwhile, creator who made a working product, then they will be more than happy to give up profits because their goal was to create the product to help people and not to make money. In giving up profits for affiliate sales, they will sell far more than they could sell on their own. As a result, their product will be available to thousands of more people. Then, when they launch another product, more people will buy it because the creator is already well-known and reputable.

Your Beginner Strategy: Don't Reinvent the Wheel

The great thing about affiliate marketing through JVZoo or ClickBank is that you can start earning nearly as much as the product creator without having to create anything. How cool is that? You can literally, promote a product and make tons of money. Of course the product creator will make more because they are collecting from multiple affiliates, but still, what a deal! There's really very little reason to spend lots of time and money creating your own product when you could simply find one that is already made. However, make sure that you find a product that works.

Saving time and money is only one big benefit of affiliate marketing. The other is the fact that the products you'll be selling will come 'pre-validated'. Pre-validation means that you will know for sure that there is a demand for the product you are selling. This is good because it also means that people will actually want to but it.

Conversely, when you create a product of your own, there's a chance that after putting all the time and effort into building it, you'll find that no one really wants it. In that case, all the marketing in the world won't help you and you'll come out of your affiliate marketing activities worse off than you started. Of course, intelligent product creators find a hole to fill, or a broken product to fix, and then create one of their own. That way, they can be sure that there are people out there who want to buy their product.

With affiliate marketing, you get to choose a product that is already selling lots of units and, in some cases, you can use their exact sales scripts in order to sell it. This is a proven quantity and as such, there's nothing that can go wrong. This is literally a 'cut and paste' business and all that's left to you is to find your own audience! In some cases, the product creator provides you with everything you need to sell their product. They want you to make sales because then they get their product out there and make some money. It is a win-win situation.

Unfortunately, many affiliate marketers don't realize this and they instead want to get clever with creating their own unique business strategy. Don't fall into this trap. Follow the cookie cutter business of affiliate marketing and you will get results. It isn't that hard. Don't make it difficult by trying to do something that won't work.

The same goes for all the people who try inventing their own new app or becoming the next massive blogger. That's all good and well but 9 times out of 10, they will fail. If you're really serious about earning money, you don't need to re-invent the wheel. Simply find what you know works and then use that exact business model to earn money yourself. Done.

This is the smartest way to start making lots of money as an affiliate marketer. Find what works and then go with it, don't try and be clever, don't be different, simply be. Once you've had some initial success and earned some cash then you can look at creating your own product or changing the world. For now, settle for earning money in a tried and tested manner, quickly and efficiently.

Believe me, I've tried. I have created several failed products, launched multiple failed affiliate sites, tried to promote products in a niche that was too big for me to be involved in, et cetera. All of the things that you are learning in this book are a direct result of years of my experience. Learn from it! It is like the old saying: do as I say, not as I do. You need to follow the simple instructions laid out in this book. Don't get clever and try your own method. It won't work. Not yet, anyway. You need to be patient, and persistent and allow your business to grow. Patience and persistence are the keys to success.

Scaling Up

Affiliate Marketing Expert

Scaling up not only works for product creators, it can also work very well for you, as an affiliate marketer. Once you have your niche and are making some money from your affiliate sales (typically about a year into your business) then you can simply employ the 'repeat what works strategy'.

The repeat what works strategy is very simple. For example, if you are making money from a certain digital product in a certain niche, then why not completely mimic that model and start selling two different digital products? That way, you can double income quickly, as well as giving yourself a backup and a more secure model as a result. All you need to do is find another related, or unrelated, digital product to promote. Then copy your exact sales model and apply it to your new product. Every few months you can add another new product and then you'll really be scaling up.

Another way to scale up without adding more products is to simply spend more money on advertising. Increase your Pay Per Click campaign, market on Facebook, send out an email campaign, or some other form of advertising. Then you will be promoting to a larger audience and, hopefully, driving more traffic to your existing affiliate marketing products. Then, monitor your own conversion rates and make sure that you are making a good return on your investment. If, after a couple of months, it is working then start increasing your budget to grow your earnings.

Basically, as an affiliate marketer, you can scale up by increasing your products, increasing your advertising, or both. However, make sure that it is worth the time and money you are investing. If after two or three months you aren't seeing the results, then it is time to change lanes. Of course, this is only after your initial year in the business. Until that year is up, you need to be patient and stick with it. Then you can only change things up after you begin to add to, and grow, your business. You will never change your initial business because the business you chose will have been chosen based upon the knowledge from this book, which came from years of experience. Therefore, it will work.

Affiliate Marketing Expert

Chapter 3:

Making Things Sell

As mentioned, there will be some cases where you can find digital products that are selling very well and that provide you with their sales page and even the e-mails they use. If you can find such a product then go for it, especially if they share their conversion rate. This removes variables from your process thereby allowing you to fine tune your business model all the more quickly. Often times, JVZoo has a page where you can see all of the conversions, returns, sales, and other rates. Make sure to choose a well-performing product that has high sales, high conversions, and low returns. That way you will know that there is a demand for the product and that the product works.

But that said, not all digital products will provide these materials, meaning that sometimes you'll still need to create your own sales page and email sequence. That is fine, as creating sales pages and emails isn't too difficult. You simply need to make sure they are worded properly, laid out correctly, and look good. In addition, there will be times when you receive sales pages and emails from a creator and you notice ways to improve upon it. It is okay to do so. You can change them up and make them your own. However, don't change it too much, because if they are providing you with sales content and they are getting a lot of sales, which they should be because you wouldn't have chosen to affiliate with them if they weren't, then that means their sales content is working.

However, should you need to create your own sales content, or wish to change someone else's content, you need to know what works and what doesn't work. That's where this section comes in: making things sell. By the end, you should know how to take your conversions from a measly 1% and boost them to a highly profitable 10%. All of this can be achieved in creating great sales content.

What is a Sales Page? Creating the Layout

The first question is: what is a sales page? The answer is that a sales page is an entire page on a website that is completely dedicated to selling one product. This means there will be no external links to other pages and no other products being promoted. The entire page is designed to draw people to the 'buy now' button and to convince them why they should, in fact, buy. The product that is being promoted is the only thing on that page. This is important. You don't even want any links to places on your site, menu bars, footers, nothing. The only links are links to buy the product. That is it.

Chances are that you will have visited sales pages in the past and you'll know them through their strange, long, multi-color design from which there is no escape. There is a lot of psychology, science, and marketing behind the creation of a sales page. During this section, most of that will be explained so that you can understand why you need to build your sales page to be so goofy.

Sales pages are generally very vertical and have a very thin passage of text that encourages lots of scrolling. This is no accident. The act of scrolling down the page makes visitors feel as though they're becoming more 'committed' to the product and the further they scroll, the less they will normally want to come away empty handed. They have invested time and effort into that page and if they close it without getting anything then they will feel like they wasted their time. This is why sales pages are so long, have videos, and have the buy button at the bottom.

In addition, there will be no navigation links and no links to other pages, for the precise reason that they distract away from the 'buy now' option. Viewers are used to seeing many links on a page. Usually, most viewers click on links within pages and navigate to other pages rather than simply typing in the web address. After all, how many people Google Facebook instead of typing in the URL? The point is, viewers have a need to click on a link. If you deprive them of that need, then by the time they get to the bottom of the page and see the only link that is there, they will be more likely to click on it. They want to click on something and if that something is a large button that says 'Click Here!' they will be delighted.

Sales pages also have embedded videos with no option to control the video. This is vital. Now, you don't necessarily need videos. However, if you have them, they need to be non-controllable. That means the pause, play, scrolling, et cetera must be disabled. This can easily be done by uploading your video to YouTube and embedding it from there onto your sales page. Within your page settings simply remove all of the options. You may also be able to do this on YouTube, but that will take a bit of research.

Anyway, people love videos. Viewers are addicted to watching things. That is why YouTube is the number one search site after Google. People would rather watch a video on how to change a battery than simply reading the three lines of text explaining it. Though this is unfortunate for people as a whole, it is very good in terms of selling your product. If you place videos on your page and have them automatically play when they come into the page view, then people will stay on your page longer. They will want to watch the video. Make sure they are brief, exciting, and to the point. You want viewers to keep moving toward the Buy Now button, not bore them with a tiring video.

Making Things Sell

Another important factor is the text. The text is very important because you must have it in plain sight. Of course, this sounds obvious, but it really is important. Choose a font that is easily readable. In addition, you want to have it be large enough to read on any device. After all, most people are on a mobile screen nowadays. In addition to having a good font, you also want to make some lines of text bold, italics, and underline. You will do this with the important aspects of your sales pitch. Another great text manipulation is to increase the sizing of certain keywords on your page. Highlighting certain words or phrases is also a great trick. This will make them stand out to the viewer. After all, most people aren't going to read your page word for word. They will only read what you tell them to read.

Therefore, use your bold, italics, underline, increased size, and highlights carefully. You will want to emphasize action words that will entice people to buy the product. In addition, emphasize words or phrases that will show the viewer what's in it for them. They don't care about supporting you. They want to get something. That is why they are on your page. People are selfish and want to feel like they got a deal. Therefore, point out all the great benefits of the product and make them feel good about buying it. Show them that they need it and can't live without it.

Finally, sales pages are very often designed to be either bright red or orange around the edges. They have color, all over the place. Believe it or not, but color psychology has a tremendous effect on whether or not people buy things. Red and orange are colors that cause the heart rate to increase and make people feel uncomfortable. These colors make people want to act quickly, to leave or to buy, which makes them more impulsive. Why do you think red cars are more expensive to insure than blue cars? It is because red is a stimulant whereas blue is calming.

So what colors should you use? You will want to use reds and oranges on places related to purchasing the product and on action words because those colors invoke a need to take action. Use yellow to highlight things on your page because yellow enhances focus. Think about it. What color are legal pads, road lines, and caution signs or tape? They are all used to get you to focus for a second. Therefore, use yellow to get your viewers to make a quick stop and focus on what you showed them. Blue is a calming color that also conveys trustworthiness. Therefore, use it in places where you are describing success stories or testimonials. Try to avoid green, as that color conveys envy or sickness. Remember Mr. Yuk? If not, Google it.

One last key thing to consider when creating your landing page is conveying trust. When someone lands on your website and sees you are selling a product, they will very often be suspicious of you. In addition, they will worry that it's a scam. People still don't like handing over their details online, and so if they think your sales page looks dodgy, they'll often leave without looking back. They don't know you, they don't know your site, and they don't care. They want a product that will be good for them and they want security when purchasing it.

Your job is to make them feel safe and secure. You need to make them believe that your site is reputable, safe, and reliable. And you need to do it in less than three seconds. That means having a good company logo, having good color schemes, and following all of the science explained above. If you do, then your page will convey the security that people need. They will then stay on your page and, once they start getting into it, they will feel committed and get to the bottom. That is why the top of your page needs to be immaculate. The middle can be okay and the bottom must be excellent.

Of course, you could always sell products on an affiliated site and use their sales pages. That way you can piggyback on the established site's credibility and hopefully still get your sale. These sites will build a sales page for you and the product will be sold directly on that site. This is a huge factor to consider when you are selling a product. You want to make sure that their sales page looks good. Evaluate it based on your knowledge and the information above. Also, consider whether or not you want to take the time to create your own sales page. Even though their pages may not be perfect, there are some great advantages to using an established site.

One of the big advantages to selling products via Amazon Associates, JVZoo, or Clickbank, is that your checkout page is directly on the website itself, which makes the buyers much more likely to trust that their personal information isn't going to get stolen. It is also likely that they already have an account with that website, so in the case of Amazon, they might even be able to use the 'buy with one click' option to save themselves a ton of time and to really encourage those impulsive buying decisions.

Whatever the case may be, the initial impression you make on visitors is going to be on whatever content you have at the top of your page. Or on your landing page, which is the page that people are directed to upon clicking on some search result link. You want the content on that page to be perfect. So, make sure you put the time and effort in to creating something that looks highly professional and trustworthy. There are several themes, plugins, and templates out there that can help you with creating a sales page. Or simply use your website theme's builder to create your own based upon the information in this section.

Remember what we said about not reinventing the wheel? Why make it more difficult for yourself when you already have the means to create something professional and proven. Another option would be to have someone create a sales page for you. You can find third-party developers on Fiverr, or almost anywhere. However, make sure that they have a good track record, and make sure you see their previous work. You need to be certain that what they make for you will work.

Generally, it will be best to either use a template or pay someone to create your sales page. Unless you are really good with web design, it will be a painstaking experience. Don't get me wrong, you can do it, but it will be difficult. So, if you want to take the time to learn how to do it, and make one yourself, I highly encourage it. However, if you are more concerned with getting up and running, then spend the money on a good theme, template, or designer and go with it. Remember, that you can purchase a theme or some other software, try it out, and if you don't like it, you can get your money back.

Therefore, I highly recommend that you purchase some software to help you create your own sales pages. If you like the software then keep it and continue using it. If you don't like it, then get your money back. Make sure you use whatever you purchase within the return time limit so that you will be able to return it if necessary. In addition, you can also create a review video of yourself using the product. You can highlight the goods and bads, and then post it on the web. If it is a good product, then you can even become an affiliate!

Writing Your Sales Script

Really though, a convincing sales page is all about your sales script. The text you use to sell your product is going to be the single biggest determining factor when it comes to your conversion rates and this is something that is highly worth taking the time to learn.

There's a lot to this though, so bear with me while I explain the ins and outs of good persuasive writing.

Grabbing Attention

Affiliate Marketing Expert

The first, and biggest, challenge when it comes to making sales is to grab the attention of your visitors. Something needs to catch their attention and communicate that there's something worth reading. In addition, they need to receive the immediate impression that they shouldn't navigate away from the site. The trouble is that all of this must be accomplished within three to five seconds or you will lose your visitors.

The unfortunate reality these days is that most people are in a rush all of the time, have lots of work to do, and don't have time to read through large amounts of text. That means you can't expect your audience to stick around unless you give them a very good reason. You need to grab them with a hook right away and then reel them in.

One of the best ways to do this is to give your sales page a narrative structure. This means you need to turn your pitch into a story that your audience can relate to. There needs to be feeling and emotion behind your sale. This is probably the single most important thing about writing text. It is something that took me years to figure out and to effectively apply. Think about it, you post on Facebook all of the time and get maybe five likes and two comments. Then you post something emotional, like your pet fish died, and you have 30 likes and 20 comments! People like to relate to something. It helps them forget about their problems and relate to yours. Therefore, use emotion.

Another reason that narrative stories are so effective

is that people always want to know how stories end. Have you ever started watching a terrible program that you don't care about, only to find yourself unable to look away until the very end? In such scenarios, you'll often watch for hours even though you aren't enjoying it! This is the power of narrative and it's a human impulse that you can use to your advantage.

Basically, by telling people that you used to be in the same position as them, you can get them interested and at the same time, you'll be much more convincing. In addition, by structuring those words into a story you will hook them and keep them reading because they want to know how the story ends. They want to know what will happen. They don't really care about you and your success. They want to relate to you and envision your success as their success. Therefore, a successful sales page boils down to three things: narration, relation, and emotion.

So, how do you go about narrating your story, getting viewers to relate to it, and then feel an emotional connection?

Well, the first thing you must do is to introduce a problem. Then offer a solution to that problem. Then you will explain how you struggled through the problem and used the solution to overcome it. Now, you want to help other people do the same so you've decided to promote this product so other people can purchase it and have great results exactly like you.

For example, if you're selling a book on abs, then the 'problem' is a lack of fitness or inability to lose weight.

Affiliate Marketing Expert

The solution, of course, is your eBook on fitness. You're going to frame all this in a first person narrative where you discuss how you were once overweight until you found this incredible strategy that they can read about in your eBook. The strategy changed your life and it can change theirs too!

Obesity, tiredness, and sluggishness are types of problems that everyone can relate to. They are emotional, well-being problems. Even if someone can't, they can still read your narrative, which will invoke the emotion of empathy. This, in turn, allows them to relate to your story, which may encourage them to purchase it while thinking of someone else.

The other type of problem is something specific and simple. It is a practical problem that offers a practical solution to fix the problem. For example, if you are selling a book on stage lighting, as mentioned earlier, then you would look for a very specific and simple problem in this niche. Perhaps a problem such as how lights can be effectively attached to trusses without having people see the connections. Then explain how you struggled with your lights until you found such and such clamp. Now set up and tear down is a breeze!

At any rate, the point is that selling a product that answers a very specific need is always a good strategy because it simplifies your job to finding people who have that problem. This should come into play when you pick your product: find a product that solves a clear and easily defined problem. However, remember to make sure that it is something that you can honestly relate to and that you enjoy relating to it. It must be something that you can write about and speak from experience. Not something that you have to make up along the way or that you hate doing.

Two more great things that will grab people's attention and keep them interested are bold statements and rhetorical questions.

Bold statements grab attention simply through their brazenness. I'm not talking about bolding the font here. I'm talking about statements that will make people drop their jaw or look twice. This could mean that you open up with an unbelievable figure, or with a controversial claim. It doesn't even have to be true. Open up with something that will catch attention and make people want to receive an explanation. Later on you will explain yourself, but initially, this is a great way to get people to stop what they're doing and to read.

Rhetorical questions work well because they force the reader to think and reflect. They know they don't have to answer the question because it is supposedly rhetorical. However, in reality, there is no such thing as a rhetorical question. By definition, a rhetorical question is a question that doesn't require an answer. However, when they are asked, everyone immediately answers them in their minds. It can't be helped! Using rhetorical questions means that readers can't simply glance over the text and let it go in one ear and out the other. Now they have to actually engage with it, and think about what it means for them. It is as if they are being forced to respond to what you are saying. This, in turn, draws them in because they feel a connection to your text.

Flow and Break Points

Exactly as you need to quickly grab attention, you also need to make sure that you hold it and don't let go. Not even for a minute. If you lose someone, it will be twice as hard to get them back as it was to initially grab their attention. This is because now they are unconsciously irritated with the fact that you lead them on and wasted their time. This is why you must have good flow.

It's very important to make sure that your text flows smoothly and without obvious breaks. The text should be so compelling that it pulls the reader from one line to the next without giving them the time to think of leaving. You've heard people say that they 'couldn't put the book down'. That is because the book had excellent flow. It pulled the reader in so that they couldn't wait to find out what was next. Flow is very, very important.

This is yet another reason for the long narrow design that so many sales pages use. It naturally encourages flow because readers have to read more lines than they would on a wider page. Therefore, they feel like they have read more because they are further down the page. To them, your text seems like it had good flow because they have moved down so far.

The same is true with short sentences and lots of space. Ideally, you want to make your content as 'skim friendly as possible', especially considering that most web users skim and don't read. That is why it is essential to play with the fonts by using bold, italics, underlines, different sizes, and highlights. People are lazy and they like to get as much information with as little effort as possible. Again, that's why they like videos. Rather than fighting the inevitability of skimming, simply use it to your advantage.

Do this by spacing out your text and also by using lots of headers. In fact, it's generally considered good practice to write your headers so that the entire narrative of the text can be discerned simply by reading the headings. It is sort of like a paragraph topic sentence. You want people to know exactly what they are getting into.

Again, this is also a reason that sales pages will often underline and bold sections.

A massive, dense block of text will always be off-putting and hard to read for someone in a hurry.

On the other hand...
Imagine text with spaced out sentences...
That uses lots of **bold** statements...
And that engages the user with a strong narrative.
That uses rhetorical questions.
How much more effective might that be?
See the difference?

How much faster were you able to read those sentences than the block of paragraph text before it? Chances are, you read it much faster. In case you aren't convinced. A massive, dense block of text will always be off-putting and hard to read for someone in a hurry. On the other hand, imagine text with spaced out sentences. That uses lots of **bold** statements. And that engages the user with a strong narrative. That uses rhetorical questions. How much more effective might that be? See the difference?

Another consideration when it comes to flow is maintaining the interest of your audience and ensuring that your content is never dull or boring. If you start repeating yourself, or if the quality of your writing drops, you can lose your readers. A good solution is to re-read the text on different days. In addition, get other people to do the same. As you're reading, identify the points where you occasionally lose interest. Then simply fix those sections by spacing them out or using more interesting language.

Finally, you can also make sure you hold attention by directly addressing any concerns of the reader. The big problem you're contending with here is people saying 'yeah, but'. If they have heard your pitch before then they'll be cynical and they won't engage with what you're saying. That's why it's your job to anticipate the problems they'll have and then answer them before they become an issue. Basically, you want to address mini problems throughout your narrative. You want to be the one to introduce the skepticism. That way they will relate to it, and then they will be more apt to relate to, and agree with, your solution.

That's why you'll often encounter the 'I know what you're thinking' line:

'I know what you're thinking – this is only another

training program that you'll never complete! You've tried countless others like it right? What makes this one any different? I had the exact same thought, but see that's where Brutal Ab Training is so effective. Because it works so quickly and because it's such a fun challenge, it is incredibly easy to stick to!'

If you can notice places where readers will become skeptical and then raise that skepticism before they can think about it. Then they will unconsciously appreciate the fact that you dissed your own product. Then, when you address the skepticism, they will be more apt to believe you because they already believed you when they agreed with your introduction of skepticism. It comes down to this: if you warn someone of a potential threat, then it doesn't take them by surprise and they don't think it was a big deal. However, if you don't warn them, then they become all freaked out and it is a big deal.

Appealing to Authority and Statistics
The 'I know what you're thinking paragraph' above would be very effective at convincing people that your product isn't like every other. But if you want to take it one step further, you can also reference statistics or authority figures. While we all know that statistics are remarkably easy to manipulate, this doesn't prevent them from being very effective tools for persuasion. In fact, statistics are one of the most powerful selling tools available. Why do you think so many companies spend so much money doing hours or research to find them? It's because they work.

Follow that last statement up with a statistic then and

you make it much more believable and convincing. For example:

'Because it works so quickly and because it's such a fun challenge, it is incredibly easy to stick to! Maybe that's why the program has a success rate of 95% across over 3,000 users!'

Equally effective would be to quote an authority figure in a related field as this can similarly lend weight and credence to your statements. Even simply quoting a user can be effective. Social influence plays such a big role in decision-making, which is why many sales pages have testimonials and reviews littered throughout the text. If you have quotes from a bunch of people singing the praises of your program, then it not only makes the program sound effective, it also makes it sound like something that's new and exciting. It gives the feeling that everyone is trying it. In turn, that greatly increases the desirability that is associated with it.

Value Proposition

When it comes to your sales page, value proposition is a very important aspect to keep in mind. A value proposition is essentially the thing that you are promising to do for your buyer via the product. This is what gives the product its value. It is what the buyer is going to get out of the product. It's the 'what's in it for them' factor.

This should be at the forefront of your sales pitch

because it is what will give the product you're selling its emotional hook. Why does that matter? Well, it is because most things that people buy are purchased based on emotion rather than logic. As the old saying goes: you don't sell a hat, you sell a warm head. It's much easier to sell a warm head because a cold head is a problem, a warm head is the desired result because it something that will make people happier and more comfortable. The hat is simply the solution to the problem.

Likewise, if you're selling an eBook on fitness then you aren't selling a book. Instead, you're selling fitness, confidence, a better love life, and any other emotional result. These are all the valuable things that having abs provides people. Selling a book on making money online? Then you're really selling financial freedom. You're really selling freedom from debt or money problems. This is a really important concept to understand because you can charge a lot more for great abs and a great love life than you can for a PDF!

This is incredibly important, as it is ultimately what is going to get your readers to really want your products rather than only being interested in them. This creates the emotion that will then lead to the snap decision to buy. As long as you've made your sales page look professional and you've provided lots of opportunities for people to click your Call To Action button.

Creating Urgency
When you get people reading your sales page, you're really trying to stir up a nice little 'neurochemical cocktail' in their brain. You want to get them to focus

using your bold statements, your narrative structure, and the problem you've outlined that needs to be solved.

You've then focused on the value proposition and you've got them imagining what life would be like with those abs, or all that money. You've told your story and conjured up their emotions and gotten them to relate to you and your product. This then creates a real sense of desire and makes the reader feel as though they must have the item that you're promoting.

Finally, you're going to create anxiety. The anxiety comes from the thought that the product won't be around forever and that it's going to disappear or go up in price. You actually have no control over whether that's true as an affiliate, but that doesn't mean your sales page can't vaguely allude to the idea that the product won't be in stock forever, or that the price will likely go up in the near future. This creates 'urgency', which, in turn, prevents the user from wanting to leave the site and 'think about it'.

You need to make sure they act now rather than later. You can do this by offering a limited time discount, as some affiliate schemes give you flexibility over the pricing, or by saying there's only limited stock and thereby creating scarcity. This also makes the product seem more popular. The bottom line is that you can't let them leave your site to think about it. 90% of the people who walk off a car lot without purchasing a car will never go back.

Removing Risk

Finally, you should also try to remove any risk associated with the product. This is important because human beings are naturally 'loss averse'. This means that people are more motivated by avoiding loss than they are by achieving gain. So if you let someone play a game where they have a 75% chance of earning $100 and a 25% chance of losing $20, they may still not play. However, if you told someone they can play for free and maybe win $10 then you would have everyone playing because they have nothing to lose. Consider this, when you win money, how long does the good feeling last? Conversely, when you lose money, how long are you broken up about it? People want to avoid loss.

When we're buying, this comes into play if we think the product might be low quality or if we think that it could be a scam. This is why you should always offer a '100% money back guarantee'. In addition, consider offering a 'try before you buy'. All the big affiliate networks offer the former. However, there may be ways you can provide the latter such as giving away the first chapter, after checking with the product creator.

One thing to keep in mind though is that people are lazy. Therefore, if you offer them a money back guarantee and get them to purchase the product, the odds of them returning it are low. This is mainly because it is easier not to go through the hassle of returning it. In the same way, if you give them a free chapter, the odds of them returning to your site and purchasing the entire book are low. This is because it is easier to simply not go back and buy the book.

Either way, providing increased security and removing the risk will help the reader feel more comfortable with purchasing the product and to negate any doubts they may have.

Chapter 4:

More Platforms for Selling

Of course, your sales page is only one place where you can promote and sell affiliate products. One other place, for instance, is within the body of your articles themselves, which will be a more passive approach.

Blog Posts

So for example, if you're running a blog and using this to create a big audience that you can drive to your sales page, you can also use those blog posts to make your sales. All you have to do to do is to embed URLs within the body of those posts. Here, you might simply mention how 'X product' is really good for whatever you're writing about and then leave the link there for a reader to click. If they're really interested in your content and you're doing a great job of demonstrating your knowledge and making it exciting, this can lead to a few extra clicks.

This is an especially good strategy to use when selling physical products as an Amazon affiliate. You can even leverage the reader's curiosity to get them to click on the product. For example, you might write an article on dating and mention how some people will even use pheromones, or oxytocin sprays, in order to make themselves more appealing and here's a great product to check out.

Would you click the link?

Clearly, this is something people might click on out of sheer curiosity even if they don't intend to buy. After all, you would probably think about clicking on the link. Hopefully, you would even click on it because, if you did, it will be easier to make my point. Humans like to click. They like to explore. Put links in your blog posts and they will get clicks. They may not get sales, but that really doesn't matter too much if you are affiliating physical products on Amazon. This is because Amazon has a 24-hour cookie, which means that you can make commission on anything that your viewers might subsequently decide to buy on the site, even if they come back later of their own accord!

Likewise, you can use links to physical products in blog

posts that are directly related to that product. A lot of bloggers make their main income from reviewing Amazon products and linking to them. Many people will read reviews of laptops, for instance, before they buy. If they follow your link, out of sheer convenience, after reading your comments, then you made an affiliate sale for reviewing the laptop.

Email Marketing

Something else that lends itself very nicely to affiliate marketing is email marketing. Simply build a large mailing list from your blog and then pitch products to them.

Of course, you'll need to create a compelling blog and give your readers a good reason to subscribe in order to build this list large enough. However, once you've done that, you'll then have direct access to a huge audience of people who trust you and who actively gave you permission to contact them.

You can now carry out your sales copy over the course of several emails. Each email can serve to build interest and anticipation for a product. At the same time, you can also provide valuable information to them via tips, entertainment, or general information. The great thing about this is that your audience will have to wait until you send them the call to action before they know how to buy. People always want what they can't have, so if you do this well, then you can build excitement for a product way before you launch it. That way, once you have the sales page completed, you will immediately have multiple people who were dying to buy whatever it is you were promoting.

Affiliate Marketing in Person

Believe it or not, you can even perform affiliate marketing in person. Alternatively, you can do it by posting flyers exactly as you might if you were selling a product or service on commission as an employee.

All you need a simple URL that people can type into their browser. This could be achieved using link cloaking or using a sales page of your own creation. However it is created, it needs to be very easy to remember and super easy to spell. From there, you can add the link to the flier and hand it out to people in the street, post it through people's doors. You can even do a pitch in person to explain why the product is so good.

This is a strategy that works particularly well for lifetime membership programs. For example, if you can find a bingo site with an affiliate program, print off some fliers, and then hand them out in an area with a large elderly population, you can quickly get some people to sign up who will subsequently earn you an income for the entire time they are members.

Notice how different strategies work better for different types of affiliate products and for different demographics? Once again, the key here is to have synergy between your product selection, your own blog, and your routes to market. Think of everything before you choose your first product!

Using Your Existing Routes to Market

As mentioned before, there's a good chance that whoever you are, you will have at least one good route to marketing. Often times, it's simply a matter of thinking hard enough and deciding that you can market to that selected group of people.

For instance, it might be that among your friends, you know someone who runs a magazine on gardening with a readership of 5,000. This is a fantastically easy route to market for you, especially as there's probably a website with a forum involved too. All you need to do is ask nicely and see if they will cover your story. Another example might be your old college paper. If you're alumni from a university with a particularly big fashion department, then this could be the perfect place to sell your eBook on 'getting into the fashion industry'.

You can market anywhere. Remember that social media is also a great tool. Start contacting all of your old friends and connections and see if they would be willing to follow your blog. See if they would sign up for your mailing list, or promote your site in some way. Maybe they will post products for you. You never know until you ask. The key is that you need to consider every possible way that you can get your product out there.

Essentially this is a form of influencer marketing. The only difference is that you're aiming for an influencer you already know versus trying desperately to find one.

Influencer Marketing

Plan B?

Try desperately to find one!

Another great way to accomplish the same thing as mentioned above is simply to find an influencer that you can work with and reach out to them. You can either pay them to give you a shoutout or you can do something in return as a favor.

A great example is to write a guest post for a blog. This is a strategy commonly used to build links to a website, but it can also be effective when used as a way to get direct sales. Find a blog that accepts contributions from other writers, then offer to write them an article for free that they can publish on their site, in exchange for including a link to your website (which is simply a landing page with your affiliate product). If you can get on a blog with hundreds of thousands of people reading, then you can potentially get your link seen by thousands overnight which can be enough to fix you up for life! Yes, sometimes it really does come down to that one link on that one key site.

How do you reach these big influencers who are leading your niche?

There are two strategies that work:
Interact with them in person – Go to networking events or even hire their services. Either way, create an actual relationship in person. Then they will be motivated to help you succeed because they know you and are connected to you. In the same way, if you mention them in your posts they will have skin in the game. Not only could they receive some business, but now they could also lose business if they fail to help you out.

Build your way up – Don't approach Tony Robbins when you have a readership of one. Instead, aim for someone much smaller and then gradually look for bigger and bigger affiliates. You should always be on a similar level with the person you're asking to help you. This way there's more likely to be something in it for them as well as you. It also means you're less likely to get laughed out of their inbox.

Affiliate Marketing Expert

Chapter 5:

Marketing Your Blog, Mailing List, and Sales Page

The above strategies are what are known in the industry as 'growth hacks'. That is to say that they're techniques you can use to quickly increase your exposure to a much wider audience, rather than to grow slowly using the normal trajectory. However, it is more likely that you'll take a more straightforward approach and gradually rise through the ranks via SEO, or Search Engine Optimization, social media, and content marketing.

The Power of Content Marketing

Content marketing means simply creating lots of value on your website by writing high-quality blog posts, articles, and features. What you write needs to be worthwhile for the reader. I know we've been over this before, but it is important. No one will subscribe to dull and boring content.

The objective is to give people a reason to visit your site, and content is the main reason people visit any website on the net. At the same time though, your content is what's going to demonstrate your knowledge and your know-how. Therefore, you need to make sure you are writing about something that you not only know about but also something about which you are passionate. This will help build trust and authority. That way any products you decide to promote will be more likely to be taken seriously by your audience.

This is also what will encourage people to sign up to your mailing list and what will make affiliates want to work with you. Generally, this is what will help you to go from 0 viewers a day to 10,000 viewers a day. Make sure that your content is long enough to offer real value (around 1,800 words according to research) and that it is unique and engaging. You can't write articles that are derivative and expect people to rush to subscribe to your mailing list!

Another tip is to make sure that you are putting in the time and effort to create as much content as possible.

The key here is that in order to make a full-time living from a blog, you need to treat it like a full-time living in terms of the work you put in. This is again why it is so important that you enjoy what you are writing about because you will need to continually find new post content and write post after post after post.

It is also important that you be on every social media site and make sure that you provide value on there as well. That way you're giving people a reason to want to follow you.

Do this consistently and you'll gradually build an audience that trusts you and that you can sell to time and time again.

Pay Per Click (PPC)

In terms of Pay Per Click advertising, there are two main networks you will likely choose from. These are Google AdWords and Facebook Ads. The former lets you place your adverts alongside specific searches right on the Search Engine Results Pages, or SERP's, the latter allows you to show ads on users' home feeds.

The great thing about both these types of advertising, other than their pay per click nature, is the fact that they let you carefully target a very specific type of visitor. Seeing as you pay for each click, your objective is not to get as many people as possible to go to your website, but rather to make sure that only the people most likely to buy from you see the ads and click on them. For obvious reasons, your goal here is sales, not clicks.

On Google AdWords, you accomplish this by targeting phrases that only your potential buyers would search for. So if you're selling a book on getting abs, you might target phrases like 'how to get abs' but use Google's 'negative keywords' tool to filter anyone who uses the term 'free' because they're not looking to buy anything. You would then put the price of your eBook right in the description alongside your ad so that only people who are likely to buy from you will consider clicking it, thereby improving your return on investment.

On Facebook, you can do something similar by targeting your readers based on their age, sex, location, job, hobbies etc. This means that if you're selling an eBook on wedding planning, you can target specifically women who are engaged. Again, this greatly reduces the number of people who will click your ads who won't be a potentially relevant customer.

Your ads need to be highly targeted and specific. You are marketing to a narrow span of people because you don't want to be paying for clicks that don't amount to anything. When you are in a pay per click campaign you need every click to count. Therefore, use as many of the criteria as you can so that your audience will be highly specialized. However, when you are simply posting on your blog, social media, or elsewhere, you want clicks. Because that will bring people to your site and you don't have to pay for that traffic. It's as simple as that.

Once more, your key to success is to think of all this before you choose your product. Ask yourself: how easily can you target your visitors?

Chapter 6:

Conclusions: The Secrets You Have Learned

So there you have it: everything you need to know to be much more effective at affiliate marketing than about 90% of people who get into it.

A lot of information has been covered and many secrets have been revealed. However, it was all done in a pretty dense manner. Hopefully, you will take the time to review the material and really learn from it. In summation, let's highlight a few of the biggest and most important tips that we've gone over.

Affiliate Marketing Takes Time

To be successful at affiliate marketing you need to approach it with the right expectations and intentions. To start with, aim to earn some money on the side. Get away from the thought that you'll be a millionaire overnight. Your goal should be to supplement your income doing something you love and in time you'll start making your riches. Remember the timeline, it will be about eighteen months to two years before you are large enough to begin to consider making affiliate marketing a career. However, if you are already a professional blog writer with thousands of followers, start with related products.

Copy and Paste Your Business

Don't reinvent the wheel. Keep it simple as much as possible. Choose a digital product that has lots of proven sales and use the exact business model as far as possible to benefit from that proven success. Employ the repeat what works strategy. Remember that there are many other people out there who run a successful affiliate marketing business. Do what they do and do as I say. Your goal is to have a good business and earn some money. Stick with the simple principles outlined here and then, much later, you can start to venture out on your own.

To scale up your business and get even more sales simply find a new product and apply the exact same format over to that one. Remember, you are going to repeat what works, not try to come up with something new.

Start Small and Climb the Ranks

If you don't have lots of money to invest in Pay Per Click, then aim for a smaller niche, to begin with. If you can find an affiliate product aimed at a particular industry that solves a specific problem, this will often be a great place to start. Then you can reinvest the money you make once you've saturated that smaller market. This will greatly improve your rankings and give you lots of authority. That way, once you move into larger niches you will have a much better chance of holding onto viewers who arrive at your page via search results.

Think About How You'll Market Before You Choose Your Product

Don't pick a product and then worry about how to reach an audience. Instead, pick a product with an idea of how you're going to sell it. You need to have a detailed plan of attack before you strike.

What is the value proposition?
What routes to market do you already have?
How easy is it to target the specific demographic?

If you follow the notions put forth in this book and use these strategies then you will be far ahead of anyone else in the game. You need to be persistent and patient and you will find that affiliate marketing really can make you rich and allow you to earn an entirely passive income. Stick with it, enjoy it, and it will happen!

Best of luck!

~Spencer Coffman

Appendix A:

Checklist

You've read the book, Affiliate Marketing Expert by Spencer Coffman, now it's time to start putting those steps and methods into action. It is do or die time, because once you start affiliate marketing, you're in it for the long haul. It's time to start setting up your business and laying the groundwork for, what could be, your retirement.

To do that, you're going to need to remember everything you've learned and put it into action. That's where the Affiliate Marketing Expert Checklist will come in handy. Work through this selection, and you should be a lot closer to achieving the kind of lifestyle you want and gaining the kind of financial security and freedom that is so elusive in the modern age.

In the full book, we discussed a large number of different techniques and strategies you can use to become highly successful at affiliate marketing. We went well beyond the 'regular' techniques used by most marketers and instead looked at advanced growth hacks and similar strategies that could help you to accelerate your growth and earn a lot more cash a lot more quickly.

But that was all very dense and a lot for you to absorb and remember all at once. Conversely then, this checklist will outline the simple steps you need to take to get to the very top of affiliate marketing. It's sort of like the basic principles of the book. You'll see how you easily can start making money by promoting another product and how easy it is for you to reach a huge audience.

Of course, this is only a checklist. You'll still need to read through the full book if you want to be as successful as you can possibly be. Anyway, here is the Affiliate Marketing Expert Checklist.

Examine Your Situation

I know you're excited to make a lot of money with affiliate marketing. However, it doesn't happen overnight. Before you begin you need to assess your lifestyle and determine whether or not you are determined to make affiliate marketing work.

- Do you have the time to dedicate two hours every other day to your business?

- Are you in need of some extra cash?

- Are you patient and willing to work more now to receive a higher payoff later?

- Do you enjoy learning and working on the computer?

- Would you like to be your own boss and be financially free in three to five years?

If you answered yes to all of these questions then you are definitely ready to start an affiliate marketing business.

Know What You're Getting Into

Before you begin an affiliate marketing business you need to make sure you are in the right mindset. Affiliate marketing isn't going to be easy. It is like any business and it takes time and work to be successful.

- Starting an affiliate marketing business is going to take time and effort.

- You are going to have to conduct a lot of research.

- You need to invest the money you make back into the business.

- It may be three to five years before you start

seeing "real" payouts.

Be Prepared For A Challenge

In the main book, you learned about many of the challenges in setting up an affiliate marketing business.

* Unless you invest a lot of money right away, you won't make huge returns right away. That means it will take time.

* For a while, you will be working a lot more with little reward.

* You are building "sweat equity" for the future.

* Expect setbacks and deal with them accordingly, don't let them stop you!

Find Your Product/Niche

In affiliate marketing, you need to decide what products you are going to promote long before you start your business. You need a detailed plan of action. Dedicate time and research to find a good niche.

* Find your product BEFORE you start anything else.

* Select a product that you know you can sell.

* Start with a smaller niche.

Checklist

o   Be very specific and honed in.

o   Try to solve a problem or provide a solution.

- Needs to be a product you like and believe in.

- Needs to be something that you know about and can write about.

- Look for something with a proven track record.

- Find another successful business model and see how you can copy it.

Develop A Marketing Plan

So you've chosen your product. It's a product that you know a lot about and absolutely love. You can write about it and aren't afraid to tell others about it. It is something that is in demand and that can help people with a problem. Now you need to decide how you are going to promote that product.

- Is is a physical or digital product? This will determine how you promote it.

- Are you going to go door to door, sell to family, friends, and co-workers?

- You need a website. Will it be your own or will you use a web 2.0.

o Get your domain name.

o Get a hosting account.

o Build your website.

o (I can help you with this aspect. Simply contact me.)

- Get yourself on social media.

    o Use your personal profiles to promote.

    o Create pages, boards, blogs, et cetera for your business.

- Consider email marketing.

Set Up Your Sales Page

A sales page is an important part of your website. You need to make sure that it is designed properly and will capture attention. Psychology and marketing play a huge role here.

- Make it long and narrow so they keep scrolling.

- Use action colors as well as trustworthy colors.

- Make sure your text is persuasive and has a strong hook.

- Relate to the reader, make them feel like you

understand them.

- Show them how they need your product.

    o   Solve a problem.

    o   Improve their life.

    o   Make things easier.

- Place nice buy buttons on the bottom of the page.

Promote

Now that everything is set up, you need to promote your page. This is where social media and other marketing strategies come into play.

- Start posting everywhere that you can.

- Write blog posts and get others to link back to you.

- Consider paid advertising on Google or Facebook.

- Use videos on your site to keep viewers engaged.

- Get some press release and magazine shout outs.

- Tell everyone you know and ask them to spread the word.

All of these tasks are much easier said than done and starting an affiliate marketing business is more work than people realize. However, the payoff is much greater than many other businesses out there. In addition, if you really dedicate yourself and have the time and effort to put in right away, you can start receiving income in a few months! It's like anything, you will get out of it what you put into it. You reap what you sow. Therefore, be willing to put in the time and effort and you will see success.

Best of Luck,

~Spencer Coffman
SpencerCoffman.com

Appendix B:

Resource Cheat Sheet

Hopefully, by now you've read the book Affiliate Marketing Expert By Spencer Coffman. If so, you know what you can do to start making some money online. Life always seems like it is filled with one expense after another. These expenses can either be really easy or really difficult depending on your monetary situation. Fortunately, you have decided to take the next step. You are dedicated to always having enough money. You've had enough of struggling to make ends meet and have decided to do something about it. Fortunately, Affiliate Marketing Expert provided you with some great ideas on how you can start making extra cash with affiliate marketing.

Therefore, make an effort to incorporate what

you learned in the book and work hard to become financially free. Of course, it is a lot easier said than done, but nothing good comes easy. If you want to live a life of financial peace then you need to make some changes. It's a mindset that you need to work to develop and it will take time and effort. Don't worry though; the Affiliate Marketing Expert Resource Cheat Sheet will help give you a leg up in the world of affiliate marketing so you can start making more money sooner, rather than later.

Resources

Warrior Special Offers

http://www.warriorforum.com/warrior-special-offers/

Warrior Forum is a great resource that you can use to find trending affiliate products and keep up with what is happening online. You can also promote affiliate products of your own. Be careful though, they have a lot of rules and you can get blocked pretty easily if you aren't careful.

CB Trends

http://www.cbtrends.com/popular-clickbank-products-1.html

This is a list that shows the top trending and popular products on ClickBank. Use it to help you decide which products you are going to promote.

Spencer Coffman YouTube Channels
https://spencercoffman.com/youtube-channels

Here are some great channels with lots of reviews for affiliate products that you may wish to use to help you with your business. Go ahead and start watching some of the videos, see how the products work, and decide which ones are best for you.

How To Cloak Your Affiliate Links
https://yoast.com/cloak-affiliate-links/

When you start promoting affiliate products it is a good idea to cloak your links so that the social media sites have a harder time recognizing them. This will help make sure your posts don't get blocked.

The Truth About Affiliate Marketing
http://spencercoffman.com/truth-about-affiliate-marketing/

This article explains the truth about affiliate marketing and tells you what you need to know before you dive into the exciting world of affiliate marketing.

Popular Affiliate Networks

JVZoo
https://www.jvzoo.com/affiliates

JVZoo is probably the best affiliate network for

beginners. You can sign up to promote any product you like by requesting approval directly from the seller. Commissions vary depending upon the seller. Go ahead and request to **promote my books and I'll give you 100% of the sale!**

ClickBank
http://www.clickbank.com/affiliate-network/

ClickBank is a pretty good affiliate network. It is more widely known that JVZoo, which means that there are tons of promotion opportunities. Unfortunately, it isn't as easy to use as JVZoo but don't let that stop you!

Commission Junction
http://www.cj.com/

Commission Junction, now known as CJ, is kind of a hassle. They have a lot of rules and the interface is convoluted. In addition, if you don't have a certain number of referrals each month, they may restrict your account. Whether or not you use it is up to you.

Amazon Associates
https://affiliate-program.amazon.com/welcome/getstarted

Amazon Associates is Amazon's affiliate program. You can sign up for free and get a link to any product on Amazon. You can also promote search results and general pages. The only trouble is Amazon doesn't like to pay its affiliates. They have rules and loopholes, which mean you rarely get credited for your referrals. Still it's worth signing up and using because once you surpass their limitations you will get paid. However, until then, it can be frustrating.

eBay Partner Network
https://partnernetwork.ebay.com/

Like Amazon, eBay also has an affiliate network. However, because they aren't as large as Amazon, they are pretty lax with the rules. Simply sign up and you can create links to any eBay item. They track your referrals and pay you for every purchase you refer, unlike Amazon, who only pays you for "qualified" purchases.

Tools For Affiliate Marketing

Pretty Link
http://spencercoffman.com/Pretty-Link-Pro-Link-Cloaker

Pretty link is a great WordPress plugin that you can use to cloak your affiliate links. I recommend the pro version because it is highly worth it. Go ahead and take a look at my review video as well.

Thrive Products
https://thrivethemes.com/

Thrive has several products that may be useful for

your affiliate marketing business. Go ahead and take a look at the many different tools they have to offer.

Great Amazon Affiliate Tools
https://www.youtube.com/playlist?list=PLT8jxlIkhNOQNR_UwBLXt52lRYY9Ce88I

Here are some amazing products that you can use to really help you build your affiliate store. There are plugins, themes, and software tools that can save you a lot of time and money.

Script Engage
http://scriptengage.io/

Script Engage is an amazing online tool that you can use to help create any type of script that you will ever need. You can make sales pages, email swipes, lead pages, landing pages, and anything and everything else!

Of course, there are many more great resources out there. However, the Affiliate Marketing Expert book, the Checklist, the Mind Map, and this Resource Cheat Sheet should be more than enough to get you started. Stick with it, and you'll start noticing some great success in no time!

SpencerCoffman.

Resource Cheat Sheet

Affiliate Marketing Expert

Appendix C:

Mind Map

Here is the list version of the Affiliate Marketing Expert Mind Map. The flow chart is located online at SpencerCoffman.com. Go ahead and check it out so you can use it to help you with your affiliate marketing business.

Examine Your Situation

Do you have the time to dedicate two hours every other day to your business?

Are you in need of some extra cash?

Are you patient and willing to work more now

to receive a higher payoff later?

Do you enjoy learning and working on the computer?

Would you like to be your own boss and be financially free in three to five years?

Know What You're Getting Into

Starting an affiliate marketing business is going to take time and effort.

You are going to have to conduct a lot of research.

You need to invest the money you make back into the business.

It may be three to five years before you start seeing "real" payouts.

Be Prepared For A Challenge

Unless you invest a lot of money right away, you won't make huge returns right away.

That means it will take time.

For a while, you will be working a lot more with little reward.

You are building "sweat equity" for the future.

Expect setbacks and deal with them accordingly, don't let them stop you!

Find Your Product/Niche

Find your product BEFORE you start anything else.

Select a product that you know you can sell.

Start with a smaller niche.

Be very specific and honed in.

Try to solve a problem or provide a solution.

Needs to be a product you like and believe in.

Needs to be something that you know about and can write about.

Look for something with a proven track record.

Find another successful business model and see how you can copy it.

Develop A Marketing Plan

Is it a physical or digital product?

This will determine how you promote

it.

Are you going to go door to door, sell to family, friends, and co-workers?

You need a website. Will it be your own or will you use a web 2.0.

Get your domain name.

Get a hosting account.

Build your website.

Get yourself on social media.

Use your personal profiles to promote.

Create pages, boards, blogs, et cetera for your business.

Consider email marketing.

Set Up Your Sales Page

Make it long and narrow so they keep scrolling.

Use action colors as well as trustworthy colors.

Make sure your text is persuasive and has a strong hook.

Relate to the reader, make them feel like you

understand them.

Show them how they need your product.

Solve a problem.

Improve their life.

Make things easier.

Place nice buy buttons on the bottom of the page.

Promote

Start posting everywhere that you can.

Write blog posts and get others to link back to you.

Consider paid advertising on Google or Facebook.

Use videos on your site to keep viewers engaged.

Get some press release and magazine shout outs.

Tell everyone you know and ask them to spread the word.

Affiliate Marketing Expert

Created by Spencer Coffman
SpencerCoffman.com

About The Author

Spencer has dedicated countless amounts of time, effort, and research learning the ins and outs of affiliate marketing. He knows what it takes to be a successful affiliate marketer and how to quickly achieve results. Read Affiliate Marketing Expert to learn how to do the same! To read more about Spencer, visit his website spencercoffman.com

Affiliate Marketing Expert

www.ingramcontent.com/pod-product-compliance
Lightning Source LLC
Chambersburg PA
CBHW051545170526
45165CB00002B/887